The American Enigma is You

Poems by Joe Dimino

Spartan
Press

Spartan Press
Kansas City, Missouri

Spartan
Press

Copyright ©Joe Dimino, 2024
First Edition: 1 3 5 7 9 10 8 6 4 2
ISBN: 978-1-958182-95-6
LCCN: 2024947701

Cover image: Jason Baldinger
Title page image: Jim McGowin
Author photo: Amanda Dimino

"I found that we may have some similarities in our backgrounds and why we write poetry. It's cathartic and therapeutic for you and your writings offers the reader the same opportunity for catharsis and therapy. I love the format of highlighting the first line and the syncopated style. The poems focus on homey, relatable topics that allows the reader to visualize the moment. You appear to appreciate the moments, the singular "epiphanies" of life. It is truly a fantastic collection."

-Russ Haddad, Author of *Growth* and *Pieces of Mind*

"Joe's words are innovative - buzzing with improvisational nostalgic imagery, much like jazz music itself. His words pulstate and pop, captivating the reader's mind and attention. Packed with wisdom, wit, and humor these poems are a delight from start to finish."

-Elena Stephenson, Author of *Pink Door* Series

"These poems are echoes of reality on a frequency that only Joe is attuned to catch and record. Joe has a way of capturing these echos of reality, be they familiar or abstract, in a way that perfectly encapsulates the spirit of the thing he'd set out to capture. I see in these poems Joe's lived reality being reflected back on him in a way that gives a narrative voice to that little person who lives on your shoulder and watches your life alongside you.

-Jon Sweetwood, Las Vegas-based Entrepreneur, Promoter, Musician & Creative

"Joe Dimino's jazz-inflected, spare observations reveal a world of lost grocery lists, blaring amusement parks, discarded furniture, and the rare precious communication on a post-it note or a mailed index card, where ordinary people wait "in patient unison/for one/extraordinary duck or goose/to break away." This writer steps out of that unison to "dream of collecting" and voice the stray hopes and dreams that may keep us going."

-Lisa B, Author of *God in Her Ruffled Dress*

"Joe Dimino is a poet who gives us riffs bright, kindly and thoughtful. He looks and listens for those singing on their instruments. He write about several pleasures: Jazz veterans; Jazz custodians; his son's ever-fanciful language on Post-It notes. He delights in a 'little pig / wagging its tiny tail / like mad / and eating everything […]'. He sees from his home the 'white-throated sparrow that sends / out these little love notes […]' , transporting his (Joe Dimino's) wife to 'another planet made / of / red / feathery / hearts.' He's a poet finding currents and snapshots of life in the everyday."

- Don Paul, Author of *The World is Turning*

Acknowledgments

Immense thanks for the inspirations & love provided
Amanda, Miles, Jilly, Jamisyn, Teri & John Christopher .. &
to all the jazz cats that have ever walked this planet.

Table of Contents:

To everyone in the 51 years of my life
who has loved me unconditionally
& showed me the magic of existing
on this glorious blue ball.

What matters the most is
how well you walk through the fire.

- Charles Bukowski

The American Enigma is You

All the old men

on stationary
& warm
exercise bikes
facing
a huge pond
being lorded over
by a local catholic church
with officious cross
are earnestly
waiting
in patient unison
for one
extraordinary
duck or goose
to break away
&
sizzle by
our silent painting
to feel
some
real natural warmth…

Zoot suited cool cats

will
come back
in space ships
to reinstate jazz cool
& dreams
of scooting
orange man
& his fake god pals
to that
burning rock in the sky
they pray to.

Miz Elizabeth

hummed in a
dignified growl that if
there was a
jazz Delorian
to go back in time,
she would
catch Sinatra
in the heydey
of unironed collars
& girls dreaming
of something sweeter than
finding a new universe.
then,
she said seeing
Armstrong and the old crooners
of the day
would round out a
nice fictitious
trip through the bell tower
of another
stack of jazz ghosts
as her hot sardines
were waiting
in the
tour bus
with another
anonymous tip

on how to survive better

with life

on that long,

cool jazz trip.

The gaggle of 3 cats

turn into
room after room
following my steps
with wagging tales
setting spells
around me
like I am
some newly anointed
middle aged man-witch
fighting off
fictional foes
in a
simple venture across my home
to get off my socks
and charge my device,
yet
cat after cat
turns into
the final harry potter adventure
only I
will get
the chance
to exclusively read.

The jazz cats never retire

as their old bones
pound at the keys
or
bellow into the horn
or
shout at the crowd
or
laughs at a false start
& in that forever
& continuous flow
of energy
that never clocks out,
I am comforted in
one of the
very few things
on this planet
of ours
that will
simply never
come to an
end.

Time after time

I see elaborate theme park rides,
big graphics on game shows,
ornate cake decorations at the store,
girl nails adorned with thick care,
yards decorated with a plethora
& fall
into a quick sand of amazement
as to how
utterly far
humans go
to entertain each other
and titillate
our desires
to ensure that
the sun
will be validated
& the moon
has
something to
reflect off of.

That therapy of a music

is made of
cotton tips,
used paint caps,
some fresh vodka,
a slightly wilted pot leaf,
yesterday's eraser bitted crossword puzzle,
tomorrow's new dime,
a 3.0 version of seattle,
the next best beach sunset,
a solid used cat,
the breath of a 2-day old,
new mints in a brightly empty ash tray,
moon rocks on mars,
inventions in the dog's cradle,
better leftovers,
a new ending,
the best beginning,
a karma made of your finest childhood dream,
the last coffee of jesus,
watching the devil become the worst sunset,
& another year on planet earth
in the pantheon of time
we can never conceive
is the dreamy
& real surly
treble clef
of
right now.

A rotating love song

blares out into space

like a golden record

made for alien lovers

in a time

that another planet

will only be able to appreciate

as the ensuing

love making

will populate another universe

of ideological notions

that will replace

the ugly

here on earth

as this little daydream

of love song

comes to a

sure,

swift

end.

The pop tart went on strike

holding

a room full of peeps

hostage

as the chocolate feds

turn up

the literal heat

while the peeps

faded

& the pop tarts

shined

in a

made for tv show

you will

likely

never

witness.

Of all of life's mysteries

I will casually stroll by
or look up & see
a flag pole
where the flag is
at half mast
& I have no idea
what it's referencing
& then realize
I've done myself a really good deed
because I haven't listened
to the news
or delved into the tragedy
of modern living
& it always makes me
feel better
because then
I get to just
wonder & make up
some kind of secret scenario
of a hero they
should really have
half-masted for.

I sometimes wonder

who fetched

that crayon scrolled note art

in a bottle

I heaved into

the cold baltic ocean

via vernazza, italy

as I fled towards america

after

9-11-01

not

real

sure

what

I wrote

here in my

50th year

on earth

&

1 pandemic down.

There's a little old man

that sits slumped over
so far
he's almost at a
50° bend
when I go to the jazz at noon series
off historic 18th & vine
while his wife sits next to him
holding his hand
& I feel the history
& lots of jazz
flowing through them
& it's the most quintessential
beautiful thing
I think that I could ever witness
in a paltry populated crowd
as the band swings
& his head moves ever slightly
to all of the thick memories
that made him
feel just right
on this here planet
of ours.

Our cat lords over me

like a rumored politician
with a vendetta
on my soul
as she curls up
by my
midnight head
licking her paws
like she is shining
gun barrels
while I
pet her tail
& promise to
get her
the shiniest badge
this side
of 9 lives.

I dream of collecting

all the strewn mattresses
& discarded love seats
& tarnished wooden chairs
smashed & smitten
on the side of the road
into an
outdoor living parlor
for the
broken & unfound
to drink free
& sleep it away
like
every broken dream
will finally
come very true.

The jazz custodians

sift & sweep
all the old
music crumbs
into the corner
that everyone ignores
but when you
accidently saunter over it
with a scotch in hand,
you leave changed
& knowing
there is
meaning
to this
once
anonymous
earth dance.

Old men driving RVs

with that
content look
on their faces
know that
nothing will ever
affect them
the way it did
when they were younger types
reminds me of
Han Solo piloting that
old glorious ship
towards the best end
of any Star Wars movie
that's never been scripted
as of yet ..

The victors of everyday democracy

cut their nails
& sharpen their memories
for the day
when a pandemic will
be forgotten
& the will
to grow old
will
once again
be safe
& hip
with
the coolest
of kids.

My son is addicted to words

on Post-It Notes
& there are bags of them
filled with great words
like
athleticism,
exhilirating,
consequentially,
frivilous
& so many more
in a cashmere of
scrabble
meets
wheel of fortune
& if you have to figure out
what he is asking for
it could be
double jeopardy
as
every day seems like
some sort
of game show
with the prize of
simple silence
or complacency.

When the corona stole my tasted buds,

I was
approached by my step-daughter
with glee
to finally
ingest those
blazing hot chips
she loves,
but i detest,
& I did it like
I had done it my whole life
as I took one after the other
with no fire,
no taste
&
the sound of
a pandemic
silently
lurching further
up our
tasty
american streets.

Every day I drive by the
Fun House Pizza

there is a

sign saying

"see you in heaven Audrey"

& now

I'm certain

she is a

carnival saint

sprinkling the

good times

right on down

into our hungry brains

like

magic

parmesan cheese.

The 665th person

meeting the
776th person
in a soup kitchen line
is like
a winning lottery ticket
waiting to explode poverty
into history
& give both the
devil and god
amoment
to simply
forget
the
battle.

The 2024 Trump chronicles

is nothing
but
a big
poem
ready to
fail,
yet lie
about how much
money it made
in a
#cancelculture
rumor
waiting
to wake you up
in the middle
of the best
sleep you had
in years.

There was a woman standing

in the middle
of a bridge off
main street
were in grandview, mo
with her hands clasped
& crying
while looking up
towards the sky
as I contemplated
whether
I should call 911
but I believed
there's a level
of her that
just needed a moment
with no one
bothering her
while she
finds her god
&
the monolith of tomorrow.

Every lost list

I find
on the ground
at stores
has
cheese
or
milk
or
ground beef
on it
proving
that
the real
earthly gods
are
cows.

I found your token

in the

bottom

of my

secret wishing well

& left it alone

like a used brick

at the trevi fountain

to ensure

that the dream

never

awakes.

Seeing all the daffodils

getting punched up
out of the ground
with their
little floppy
yellow hats
going about
are some kind
of a small miracle
here in the
new spring
that is forgetting
winter
even happened.

The entire top camper shell

from a truck

is lying

in tatters

off the side of the road

& I again wonder

who in their

right and wrong mind

wouldn't hear the

cacophony of clatter

as it fell

onto the pavement going

well over 60 mph

&wouldn't know coming home

as

their Karen yells,

"Richard .. where the hell is the top of your truck cab?"

as distant echoes

of hyena yelps

rise

& fall

in discordant unison.

The old community center maintenance man

just wants

a good book

& a hot meatball sub

as the tv

screams

for us

to take the drug

&

run as fast as

we can

towards the sun

as tonight

Saturn hides again.

I tried making a poem

out of the

long

& extra small

scrunched tall

of the Wal-Mart

pharmacy disclaimer

&

got lost

in the clauses

&

side effects.

Probably a good idea

to have

a cry

or two

every once in a while

so

I'm going

to convince

my work mates

to hoist me

on their shoulders

& carry me

out of work

like the ending of

the movie rudy

every once

in a while

to beat

that

emotional drum

correctly.

The ancient mystery of your eyes

is the smile you

forgot

as the hot air balloon leaves earth

to sprinkle the

ashes

of your

finest dreams

to grow

over and over

again

in the

groundhog's shadow.

Of all the acceptance letters

and grand yes'

I have gotten

in this life

my favorite missive

was a rejection email

from

two1361@aol.com

on Sat, Jun 13, 2015 at 11:53 pm

that read:

Joe, hello.

thanks for the interest.

I am really jammed with work and can't do anything

more than I am now

but thanks all the same.

-Henry (Rollins)

I can go weeks

and weeks
without seeing anybody
riding a bike
or jogging
or walking outside
but the minute it starts raining
there is always
that one guy
jogging through
the torrential rain
like it's dry as a bone outside
or that one guy
on a bike smiling wide
as I wonder
what is this sickness
coming from the clouds
making everyone
laugh at John Lennon
because they indeed are
not melting
in this
dry,
dry land
of ours.

Getting the notes

on index cards
& handwritten pieces
in the mail
is probably
my favorite thing
in the entire world
as they
continue to oscillate
about my orbit
like that kid
in the summertime
with my best friend Billy
waiting for
that miracle
signed baseball card
to come in
the hallowed
childhood mailbox
off Ridge street.

The early morning man

in his faded
Royals 2015
championship shirt
looks straight
into the sun
drinking his coffee
as his dog
is yanking his arm
as he slowly fades away
into a stick figure
getting pulled off
like a championship moment
we are
slowly forgetting.

Sitting outside in the parking lot

of our local amusement park
sounds like every
slasher movie
& low rent porn film
minced together
on a
mash of intrigue
&
horror
wrapped up
into
the folds
of a
subconscious
awakening.

Driving by the field out yonder

I look
at the little pig
wagging his tiny tail
like mad
as he eats everything around
just living
his best life
like he's
the penultimate
instagram star
we have
spent a
lifetime
seeking.

I saw a sign the other day

for a school district hiring bus drivers
& I wondered
if they made a typo
instead of it
being $18.25 an hour,
it was $1,825.00 an hour
& they had to honor their typo
& these bus drivers
finally started
rolling around
like aging
rock stars
parading on a yellow stage
if for only one
victorious
non/mistaken day.

My wife

Is constantly

getting

serenaded by a

neighborhood

white throated sparrow

that sends

out these

little love notes

making her feel like

she's on another planet

made

of

red

feathery

hearts.

Someone said

an amen

that will

echo

forever

& through

every human

that ever lived

&

who

did

this

we will

know finally

when the

big,

thick book

collapses to

a close...

Joe Dimino has been writing in a variety of capacities since his college days at the University of Missouri- Kansas City beginning in 1993. If you are keeping score, that would be about 30+ years. It all began at UMKCs University News as a Sports Writer with the esteemed John Beaudoin and turned into a myriad of expressive avenues, including poetry. Inventing poems has always been a therapeu/c avenue of expression. Over the long haul, he has been published in *The Thorny Locust, I-70 Review, Poetry Motel, The California Quarterly* and other online publications. These days he's a Husband, Father, IT Professional, Jazz Radio Host, Podcaster, Visual Artist & Writer. His breadth of work can be enjoyed at www.joedimino.com. If you fancy it, please reach out with any thoughts or comments at joe@ joedimino.com We highly encourage it...

This project was made possible, in part, by generous support from the Osage Arts Community.

Osage Arts Community provides temporary time, space and support for the creation of new artistic works in a retreat format, serving creative people of all kinds — visual artists, composers, poets, fiction and nonfiction writers. Located on a 152-acre farm in an isolated rural mountainside setting in Central Missouri and bordered by ¾ of a mile of the Gasconade River, OAC provides residencies to those working alone, as well as welcoming collaborative teams, offering living space and workspace in a country environment to emerging and mid-career artists. For more information, visit us at www.osageac.org

Osage Arts Community

www.ingramcontent.com/pod-product-compliance
Lightning Source LLC
Chambersburg PA
CBHW031257120626
46545CB00007B/2857